A LOVER'S COMPLAINT

By

WILLIAM SHAKESPEARE

First published in 1609

This edition is published by Classic Books Library
an imprint of Read Books Ltd.
Copyright © 2018 Read Books Ltd.
This book is copyright and may not be
reproduced or copied in any way without
the express permission of the publisher in writing

British Library Cataloguing-in-Publication Data
A catalogue record for this book is available
from the British Library

CONTENTS

William Shakespeare 5

A LOVER'S COMPLAINT 11

TO THE MEMORY OF MY BELOVED
  THE AUTHOR, MR. WILLIAM SHAKESPEARE
By BEN JONSON..................................... 25

WILLIAM SHAKESPEARE

William Shakespeare, as any reader of this book will presumably know, was an English poet, playwright and actor, widely regarded as the greatest writer in the English language - and the world's pre-eminent dramatist. His plays have been translated into every major living language and are performed more often than those of any other playwright. Referred to as England's national poet, and the 'Bard of Avon', his extant works, including some collaborations, consist of about 38 plays, 154 sonnets, two long narrative poems, and a few other verses, (some with unconfirmed authorship). Few records of Shakespeare's private life survive, and there has been considerable speculation about matters as wide ranging as his physical appearance, sexuality and religious beliefs.

William Shakespeare was the son of John Shakespeare, an alderman and a successful glover originally from Snitterfield, and Mary Arden, the daughter of an affluent landowning farmer. He was born in Stratford-upon-Avon and baptised there on 26th April 1564. His actual date of birth remains unknown, but is traditionally observed on 23rd April, Saint George's Day. Although no attendance records for the period survive, biographers agree that Shakespeare was probably educated at the King's New School in Stratford, a free school chartered in 1553, about a quarter-mile from his home. Grammar schools varied in quality during the Elizabethan era, but grammar school curricula were largely similar. Basic Latin education had been standardised by royal decree, and the school would have provided an intensive education in grammar based upon Latin classical authors.

At the age of eighteen, Shakespeare married the twenty-six year old Anne Hathaway (who was pregnant at the time), with whom he had three children: Susanna, and twins, Hamnet and Judith. After the birth of the twins, Shakespeare left few historical traces until he is mentioned as part of the London theatre scene in 1592. The exception is the appearance of his name in the 'complaints bill' of a law case before the Queen's Bench court at Westminster, dated Michaelmas Term 1588 and 9th October 1589. Between 1585 and 1592, he began a successful career in London as an actor, writer, and part-owner of a playing company called the Lord Chamberlain's Men, later known as the King's Men. By 1598, his name had become enough of a selling point to appear on the title pages.

Shakespeare continued to act in his own and in other plays after his success as a playwright. The 1616 edition of Ben Jonson's *Works* names him on the cast lists for *Every Man in His Humour* (1598) and *Sejanus His Fall* (1603). During this time, Shakespeare divided his time between London and Stratford, and in 1596 bought 'New Place' as his family home in Stratford, whilst retaining a property in Bishopsgate, North of the river Thames. He moved across the river to Southwark by 1599, the year his company constructed the Globe Theatre there. By 1604, Shakespeare had moved north of the river again, to an area north of St Paul's Cathedral with many fine houses. He appears to have retired to Stratford around 1613 at the age of forty-nine, where he died three years later.

Shakespeare produced most of his known work between 1589 and 1613. His early plays were mainly comedies and histories, genres he raised to the peak of sophistication and artistry by the end of the sixteenth century. The first recorded works of Shakespeare are *Richard III* and the three parts of *Henry VI*, written in the early 1590s during a vogue for historical drama. Shakespeare's plays are difficult to date however, and studies of the texts suggest that *Titus Andronicus, The Comedy of Errors, The Taming of the Shrew* and *The Two Gentlemen of Verona* may also belong to Shakespeare's earliest period. Shakespeare's early classical and Italianate comedies, containing tight double plots and precise comic sequences, give way in the mid-1590s to the romantic atmosphere of his greatest comedies. *A Midsummer Night's Dream,* one of his earliest comedies, is a witty mixture of romance, fairy magic, and comic lowlife scenes. The wit and wordplay of *Much Ado About Nothing,* the charming rural setting of *As You Like It,* and the lively merrymaking of *Twelfth Night* complete the sequence of great comedies.

Shakespeare then wrote mainly tragedies until about 1608. Many critics believe that his greatest tragedies represent the peak of his art. The titular hero of one of Shakespeare's most famous tragedies, *Hamlet,* has probably been discussed more than any other character, especially for his famous soliloquy beginning; 'To be or not to be; that is the question.' Unlike the introverted Hamlet, whose fatal flaw is hesitation, the heroes of the tragedies that followed, Othello and King Lear, are undone by hasty errors of judgement. In *Othello,* the villain Iago stokes Othello's sexual jealousy to the point where he murders the innocent wife who loves him. In *King Lear,* the old king commits the tragic error of giving up his powers, initiating the events which lead to the torture and blinding of the Earl of Gloucester and the murder of Lear's youngest daughter Cordelia. According to the critic Frank Kermode, 'the play-offers neither its good characters nor its audience any relief from its cruelty.' In *Macbeth,* the shortest and most compressed of Shakespeare's tragedies, uncontrollable ambition incites Macbeth and his wife, Lady Macbeth, to murder the rightful king and usurp the throne, until their own guilt destroys them in turn. His last major tragedies, *Antony and Cleopatra* and *Coriolanus,* contain some of Shakespeare's finest poetry.

Many of Shakespeare's plays were published in editions of varying quality and accuracy during his lifetime. His sonnets were published as a collection in 1609. Scholars are not certain when each of the 154 sonnets was composed, but evidence suggests that Shakespeare wrote poetry throughout his career for a private readership. In 1623, John Heminges and Henry Condell, two friends and fellow actors of Shakespeare, published the First Folio, a collected edition of his dramatic works that included all but two of the plays now recognised as Shakespeare's. It was prefaced with a poem by Ben Jonson, in which Shakespeare is hailed, presciently, as 'not of an age, but for all time.' Shakespeare was a respected poet and playwright in his own day, but his reputation did not rise to its present heights until the nineteenth century. The Romantics, in particular, acclaimed Shakespeare's genius, and the Victorians worshipped Shakespeare with a reverence that George Bernard Shaw called 'bardolatry'. His plays remain immensely popular and are constantly studied, performed, and reinterpreted in diverse cultural and political contexts throughout the world.

Shakespeare died on 23rd April 1616 and was survived by his wife and two daughters. He was buried in the chancel of the Holy Trinity Church (Stratford-upon-Avon) two days after his death, with a curse against moving his bones. The epitaph on his gravestone reads:

> *Good friend, for Jesus' sake forbear,*
> *To dig the dust enclosed here.*
> *Blessed be the man that spares these stones,*
> *And cursed be he that moves my bones.*

A LOVER'S COMPLAINT

By

WILLIAM SHAKESPEARE

A LOVER'S COMPLAINT

From off a hill whose concave womb re-worded
A plaintful story from a sistering vale,
My spirits to attend this double voice accorded,
And down I laid to list the sad-tun'd tale;
Ere long espied a fickle maid full pale,
Tearing of papers, breaking rings a-twain,
Storming her world with sorrow's wind and rain.

Upon her head a platted hive of straw,
Which fortified her visage from the sun,
Whereon the thought might think sometime it saw
The carcase of a beauty spent and done.
Time had not scythed all that youth begun,
Nor youth all quit; but, spite of Heaven's fell rage
Some beauty peeped through lattice of sear'd age.

Oft did she heave her napkin to her eyne,
Which on it had conceited characters,
Laund'ring the silken figures in the brine
That season'd woe had pelleted in tears,
And often reading what contents it bears;
As often shrieking undistinguish'd woe,
In clamours of all size, both high and low.

Sometimes her levell'd eyes their carriage ride;
As they did battery to the spheres intend;
Sometime diverted their poor balls are tied
To th' orbed earth; sometimes they do extend
Their view right on; anon their gazes lend
To every place at once, and nowhere fix'd,
The mind and sight distractedly commix'd.

Her hair, nor loose nor tied in formal plat,
Proclaim'd in her a careless hand of pride;
For some, untuck'd, descended her sheav'd hat,
Hanging her pale and pined cheek beside;
Some in her threaden fillet still did bide,
And, true to bondage, would not break from thence,
Though slackly braided in loose negligence.

A thousand favours from a maund she drew
Of amber, crystal, and of beaded jet,
Which one by one she in a river threw,
Upon whose weeping margent she was set;
Like usury applying wet to wet,
Or monarchs' hands, that lets not bounty fall
Where want cries 'some,' but where excess begs all.

Of folded schedules had she many a one,
Which she perus'd, sigh'd, tore, and gave the flood;
Crack'd many a ring of posied gold and bone,
Bidding them find their sepulchres in mud;
Found yet mo letters sadly penn'd in blood,
With sleided silk feat and affectedly
Enswath'd, and seal'd to curious secrecy.

These often bath'd she in her fluxive eyes,
And often kiss'd, and often 'gan to tear;
Cried, 'O false blood, thou register of lies,
What unapproved witness dost thou bear!
Ink would have seem'd more black and damned here!'
This said, in top of rage the lines she rents,
Big discontent so breaking their contents.

A reverend man that grazed his cattle nigh,
Sometime a blusterer, that the ruffle knew
Of court, of city, and had let go by
The swiftest hours, observed as they flew,
Towards this afflicted fancy fastly drew;
And, privileg'd by age, desires to know
In brief, the grounds and motives of her woe.

So slides he down upon his grained bat,
And comely-distant sits he by her side;
When he again desires her, being sat,
Her grievance with his hearing to divide:
If that from him there may be aught applied
Which may her suffering ecstasy assuage,
'Tis promised in the charity of age.

'Father,' she says, 'though in me you behold
The injury of many a blasting hour,
Let it not tell your judgement I am old;
Not age, but sorrow, over me hath power:
I might as yet have been a spreading flower,
Fresh to myself, if I had self-applied
Love to myself, and to no love beside.

'But woe is me! too early I attended
A youthful suit (it was to gain my grace)
Of one by nature's outwards so commended,
That maiden's eyes stuck over all his face:
Love lack'd a dwelling and made him her place;
And when in his fair parts she did abide,
She was new lodg'd and newly deified.

'His browny locks did hang in crooked curls;
And every light occasion of the wind
Upon his lips their silken parcels hurls.
What's sweet to do, to do will aptly find:
Each eye that saw him did enchant the mind;
For on his visage was in little drawn,
What largeness thinks in paradise was sawn.

'Small show of man was yet upon his chin;
His phoenix down began but to appear,
Like unshorn velvet, on that termless skin,
Whose bare out-bragg'd the web it seemed to wear:
Yet show'd his visage by that cost more dear;
And nice affections wavering stood in doubt
If best were as it was, or best without.

His qualities were beauteous as his form,
For maiden-tongued he was, and thereof free;
Yet if men mov'd him, was he such a storm
As oft 'twixt May and April is to see,
When winds breathe sweet, unruly though they be.
His rudeness so with his authoriz'd youth
Did livery falseness in a pride of truth.

'Well could he ride, and often men would say
That horse his mettle from his rider takes:
Proud of subjection, noble by the sway,
What rounds, what bounds, what course, what stop he makes!
And controversy hence a question takes,
Whether the horse by him became his deed,
Or he his manage by the well-doing steed.

'But quickly on this side the verdict went;
His real habitude gave life and grace
To appertainings and to ornament,
Accomplish'd in himself, not in his case,:
All aids, themselves made fairer by their place,
Came for additions; yet their purpos'd trim
Pierc'd not his grace, but were all grac'd by him.

'So on the tip of his subduing tongue
All kind of arguments and question deep,
All replication prompt, and reason strong,
For his advantage still did wake and sleep:
To make the weeper laugh, the laugher weep,
He had the dialect and different skill,
Catching all passions in his craft of will;

'That he did in the general bosom reign
Of young, of old; and sexes both enchanted,
To dwell with him in thoughts, or to remain
In personal duty, following where he haunted:
Consents bewitch'd, ere he desire, have granted;
And dialogued for him what he would say,
Ask'd their own wills, and made their wills obey.

'Many there were that did his picture get,
To serve their eyes, and in it put their mind;
Like fools that in the imagination set
The goodly objects which abroad they find
Of lands and mansions, theirs in thought assign'd;
And labouring in mo pleasures to bestow them,
Than the true gouty landlord which doth owe them:

'So many have, that never touch'd his hand,
Sweetly suppos'd them mistress of his heart.
My woeful self, that did in freedom stand,
And was my own fee-simple, (not in part,)
What with his heart in youth, and youth in art,
Threw my affections in his charmed power,
Reserv'd the stalk, and gave him all my flower.

'Yet did I not, as some my equals did,
Demand of him, nor being desired yielded;
Finding myself in honour so forbid,
With safest distance I mine honour shielded:
Experience for me many bulwarks builded
Of proofs new-bleeding, which remain'd the foil
Of this false jewel, and his amorous spoil.

'But ah! who ever shunn'd by precedent
The destin'd ill she must herself assay?
Or force'd examples, 'gainst her own content,
To put the by-pass'd perils in her way?
Counsel may stop awhile what will not stay;
For when we rage, advice is often seen
By blunting us to make our wills more keen.

'Nor gives it satisfaction to our blood,
That we must curb it upon others' proof,
To be forbod the sweets that seems so good,
For fear of harms that preach in our behoof.
O appetite, from judgement stand aloof!
The one a palate hath that needs will taste,
Though reason weep, and cry It is thy last.

'For further I could say, This man's untrue,
And knew the patterns of his foul beguiling;
Heard where his plants in others' orchards grew,
Saw how deceits were gilded in his smiling;
Knew vows were ever brokers to defiling;
Thought characters and words, merely but art,
And bastards of his foul adulterate heart.

'And long upon these terms I held my city,
Till thus he 'gan besiege me: Gentle maid,
Have of my suffering youth some feeling pity,
And be not of my holy vows afraid:
That's to you sworn, to none was ever said;
For feasts of love I have been call'd unto,
Till now did ne'er invite, nor never woo.

'All my offences that abroad you see
Are errors of the blood, none of the mind;
Love made them not; with acture they may be,
Where neither party is nor true nor kind:
They sought their shame that so their shame did find;
And so much less of shame in me remains,
By how much of me their reproach contains.

'Among the many that mine eyes have seen,
Not one whose flame my heart so much as warm'd,
Or my affection put to the smallest teen,
Or any of my leisures ever charm'd:
Harm have I done to them, but ne'er was harmed;
Kept hearts in liveries, but mine own was free,
And reign'd, commanding in his monarchy.

'Look here what tributes wounded fancies sent me,
Of paled pearls and rubies red as blood;
Figuring that they their passions likewise lent me
Of grief and blushes, aptly understood
In bloodless white and the encrimson'd mood;
Effects of terror and dear modesty,
Encamp'd in hearts, but fighting outwardly.

'And, lo! behold these talents of their hair,
With twisted metal amorously empleach'd,
I have receiv'd from many a several fair,
(Their kind acceptance weepingly beseech'd,)
With the annexions of fair gems enrich'd,
And deep-brain'd sonnets that did amplify
Each stone's dear nature, worth, and quality.

'The diamond, why 'twas beautiful and hard,
Whereto his invis'd properties did tend;
The deep-green emerald, in whose fresh regard
Weak sights their sickly radiance do amend;
The heaven-hued sapphire and the opal blend
With objects manifold; each several stone,
With wit well blazon'd, smil'd, or made some moan.

'Lo! all these trophies of affections hot,
Of pensiv'd and subdued desires the tender,
Nature hath charg'd me that I hoard them not,
But yield them up where I myself must render,
That is, to you, my origin and ender:
For these, of force, must your oblations be,
Since I their altar, you enpatron me.

'O then advance of yours that phraseless hand,
Whose white weighs down the airy scale of praise;
Take all these similes to your own command,
Hallow'd with sighs that burning lungs did raise;
What me your minister, for you obeys,
Works under you; and to your audit comes
Their distract parcels in combined sums.

'Lo! this device was sent me from a nun,
Or sister sanctified of holiest note;
Which late her noble suit in court did shun,
Whose rarest havings made the blossoms dote;
For she was sought by spirits of richest coat,
But kept cold distance, and did thence remove
To spend her living in eternal love.

'But O, my sweet, what labour is't to leave
The thing we have not, mastering what not strives?
Paling the place which did no form receive,
Playing patient sports in unconstrained gyves:
She that her fame so to herself contrives,
The scars of battle 'scapeth by the flight,
And makes her absence valiant, not her might.

'O pardon me, in that my boast is true:
The accident which brought me to her eye,
Upon the moment did her force subdue,
And now she would the caged cloister fly:
Religious love put out religion's eye:
Not to be tempted, would she be immur'd,
And now, to tempt all, liberty procur'd.

'How mighty then you are, O hear me tell!
The broken bosoms that to me belong
Have emptied all their fountains in my well,
And mine I pour your ocean all among:
I strong o'er them, and you o'er me being strong,
Must for your victory us all congest,
As compound love to physic your cold breast.

'My parts had pow'r to charm a sacred nun,
Who, disciplin'd and dieted in grace,
Believ'd her eyes when they t oassail begun,
All vows and consecrations giving place.
O most potential love! vow, bond, nor space,
In thee hath neither sting, knot, nor confine,
For thou art all, and all things else are thine.

'When thou impressest, what are precepts worth
Of stale example? When thou wilt inflame,
How coldly those impediments stand forth,
Of wealth, of filial fear, law, kindred, fame!
Love's arms are peace, 'gainst rule, 'gainst sense, 'gainst shame.
And sweetens, in the suffering pangs it bears,
The aloes of all forces, shocks and fears.

'Now all these hearts that do on mine depend,
Feeling it break, with bleeding groans they pine,
And supplicant their sighs to your extend,
To leave the battery that you make 'gainst mine,
Lending soft audience to my sweet design,
And credent soul to that strong-bonded oath,
That shall prefer and undertake my troth.

'This said, his watery eyes he did dismount,
Whose sights till then were levell'd on my face;
Each cheek a river running from a fount
With brinish current downward flow'd apace:
O, how the channel to the stream gave grace!
Who, glaz'd with crystal, gate the glowing roses
That flame through water which their hue encloses.

'O father, what a hell of witchcraft lies
In the small orb of one particular tear!
But with the inundation of the eyes
What rocky heart to water will not wear?
What breast so cold that is not warmed here?
O cleft effect! cold modesty, hot wrath,
Both fire from hence and chill extincture hath.

'For lo! his passion, but an art of craft,
Even there resolv'd my reason into tears;
There my white stole of chastity I daff'd,
Shook off my sober guards, and civil fears;
Appear to him, as he to me appears,
All melting; though our drops this difference bore:
His poison'd me, and mine did him restore.

'In him a plenitude of subtle matter,
Applied to cautels, all strange forms receives,
Of burning blushes or of weeping water,
Or swooning paleness; and he takes and leaves,
In either's aptness, as it best deceives,
To blush at speeches rank, to weep at woes,
Or to turn white and swoon at tragic shows;

'That not a heart which in his level came
Could scape the hail of his all-hurting aim,
Showing fair nature is both kind and tame;
And, veil'd in them, did win whom he would maim:
Against the thing he sought he would exclaim;
When he most burned in heart-wish'd luxury,
He preach'd pure maid and prais'd cold chastity.

'Thus merely with the garment of a Grace
The naked and concealed fiend he cover'd,
That the unexperienc'd gave the tempter place,
Which, like a cherubin, above them hover'd.
Who, young and simple, would not be so lover'd?
Ay me! I fell, and yet do question make
What I should do again for such a sake.

'O, that infected moisture of his eye,
O, that false fire which in his cheek so glow'd,
O, that forc'd thunder from his heart did fly,
O, that sad breath his spongy lungs bestow'd,
O, all that borrow'd motion, seeming ow'd,
Would yet again betray the fore-betray'd,
And new pervert a reconciled maid.'

TO THE MEMORY OF MY BELOVED
THE AUTHOR,
MR. WILLIAM SHAKESPEARE

By BEN JONSON

First published in 1623 as part of the preface to Shakespeare's First Folio

To draw no envy, Shakespeare, on thy name,
Am I thus ample to thy book and fame;
While I confess thy writings to be such
As neither man nor muse can praise too much;
'Tis true, and all men's suffrage. But these ways
Were not the paths I meant unto thy praise;
For seeliest ignorance on these may light,
Which, when it sounds at best, but echoes right;
Or blind affection, which doth ne'er advance
The truth, but gropes, and urgeth all by chance;
Or crafty malice might pretend this praise,
And think to ruin, where it seem'd to raise.
These are, as some infamous bawd or whore
Should praise a matron; what could hurt her more?
But thou art proof against them, and indeed,
Above th' ill fortune of them, or the need.
I therefore will begin. Soul of the age!
The applause, delight, the wonder of our stage!
My Shakespeare, rise! I will not lodge thee by
Chaucer, or Spenser, or bid Beaumont lie

TO THE MEMORY OF MY BELOVED

A little further, to make thee a room:
Thou art a monument without a tomb,
And art alive still while thy book doth live
And we have wits to read and praise to give.
That I not mix thee so, my brain excuses,
I mean with great, but disproportion'd Muses,
For if I thought my judgment were of years,
I should commit thee surely with thy peers,
And tell how far thou didst our Lyly outshine,
Or sporting Kyd, or Marlowe's mighty line.
And though thou hadst small Latin and less Greek,
From thence to honour thee, I would not seek
For names; but call forth thund'ring Aeschylus,
Euripides and Sophocles to us;
Pacuvius, Accius, him of Cordova dead,
To life again, to hear thy buskin tread,
And shake a stage; or, when thy socks were on,
Leave thee alone for the comparison
Of all that insolent Greece or haughty Rome
Sent forth, or since did from their ashes come.
Tri'umph, my Britain, thou hast one to show
To whom all scenes of Europe homage owe.
He was not of an age but for all time!
And all the Muses still were in their prime,
When, like Apollo, he came forth to warm
Our ears, or like a Mercury to charm!
Nature herself was proud of his designs
And joy'd to wear the dressing of his lines,
Which were so richly spun, and woven so fit,
As, since, she will vouchsafe no other wit.
The merry Greek, tart Aristophanes,
Neat Terence, witty Plautus, now not please,
But antiquated and deserted lie,
As they were not of Nature's family.
Yet must I not give Nature all: thy art,

THE AUTHOR, MR. WILLIAM SHAKESPEARE

My gentle Shakespeare, must enjoy a part.
For though the poet's matter nature be,
His art doth give the fashion; and, that he
Who casts to write a living line, must sweat,
(Such as thine are) and strike the second heat
Upon the Muses' anvil; turn the same
(And himself with it) that he thinks to frame,
Or, for the laurel, he may gain a scorn;
For a good poet's made, as well as born;
And such wert thou. Look how the father's face
Lives in his issue, even so the race
Of Shakespeare's mind and manners brightly shines
In his well-turned, and true-filed lines;
In each of which he seems to shake a lance,
As brandish'd at the eyes of ignorance.
Sweet Swan of Avon! what a sight it were
To see thee in our waters yet appear,
And make those flights upon the banks of Thames,
That so did take Eliza and our James!
But stay, I see thee in the hemisphere
Advanc'd, and made a constellation there!
Shine forth, thou star of poets, and with rage
Or influence, chide or cheer the drooping stage;
Which, since thy flight from hence, hath mourn'd like night,
And despairs day, but for thy volume's light.

www.ingramcontent.com/pod-product-compliance
Lightning Source LLC
LaVergne TN
LVHW041313080426
835510LV00009B/972